1 & 2

THESSALONIANS:

DISPENSATIONALLY CONSIDERED

A GRACE EXPOSITIONAL COMMENTARY

SECOND EDITION

DR. DAVID ALAN GREENE

GraceWord Publishing, LLC
www.gracewordpublishing.com
U.S.A.

GRACEWORD PUBLISHING

Contents

To My Grandsons Brayden and Casey

And the very God of peace sanctify you wholly;
and I pray God your whole spirit and soul
and body be preserved blameless
unto the coming of our Lord Jesus Christ.
Faithful is he that calleth you,
who also will do it.

- Apostle Paul

Acknowledgements

I would like to express my gratitude to Jon and Susan McMahon for their continued encouragement. A special thanks is given to Barbara Pennington and Frances Greene who worked together to proofread the manuscript.

Introduction

There is an approach to understanding Scripture that puts the entire Bible into a simple system of interpretation. The argument is that to understand God's Word we must reason from the general to the specific and not from the specific to the general. To choose a book like Thessalonians and read it apart from its biblical context would be looking at the specific outside the general structure of Scripture. This is what gets people in trouble.

God has created a timeline and eternal plan for the restoration of His Creation. This plan was first mentioned in Genesis. It is known as the *protoevangelium* or the first announcement of good news. Genesis 3:15:

> 15 **And I will put enmity between thee and the woman, and between thy seed and <u>her seed</u>; it shall bruise thy head, and thou shalt bruise his heel.**

Here, the word *seed* is singular. It refers to *the Seed* Who is Christ. Also, notice that it is the woman's seed because it was given to her by God. This is called the *immaculate conception* or the divine impregnation of the virgin Mary with the holy *Seed.* Beginning with this first promise of good news, it is said a scarlet thread is woven throughout the Bible. It is this Seed Who will redeem Creation.

God does things methodically and works His plan of restoration. He makes Himself known to man through a series of progressive revelations. Paul has a student teacher named Timothy. The letters to Timothy and Titus are referred to as the pastoral epistles because he is instructing them. Paul wants Timothy to understand and teach Scripture correctly so that he will not be ashamed or embarrassed. 2 Timothy 2:15:

> 15 <u>Study to shew thyself approved</u> unto God, a workman that needeth not to be ashamed, <u>rightly dividing the word of truth.</u>

The Greek word translated as *rightly dividing* is *orthotomeo.* It is a compound word comprised of *ortho* which mean *correct* or with *great precision* and *tomeo* which means *to cut.* As examples, *orthodox* means *correct doctrine.* Any medical procedure with the suffix

-ectomy (Gr. ek + tomeo) means *to cut out.*

This does not provide a total understanding, but when applied, it makes a huge difference. As with most things, the Bible is the sum of its parts. These parts or divisions of the Bible are referred to as *dispensations.* In Greek, the word is *oikonomia.* It also is a compound word of *oikos* meaning *household* and *nomos* which means *law or rule.* Consider the present-day meaning of the word *administration.* A president rules or administrates the country by certain laws. Therefore, a *dispensation* is a period of time in which God *dispenses* the administration of His household.

A brief summary of the dispensations does not do the subject justice. I would recommend *Letters To Theophilus* which handles the subject in greater detail. However, because it is critical to one's understanding the Bible, consider the following synopsis. Presently, we are in what some call the Church Age. However, I would not use this name because the word *church* has many uses. I prefer the name Age of Grace because that is its core message. Paul is the only one who uses the word *dispensation* in the Bible. It is used in the following four verses.

1 Corinthians 9:17:

17 For if I do this thing willingly, I have a reward: but if against my will, <u>a dispensation of the gospel is committed unto me</u>.

Ephesians 1:10:

10 That in <u>the dispensation of the fulness of times</u> he might gather together in one all things in Christ, both which are in heaven, and which are on earth; even in him:

Ephesians 3:2:

2 If ye have heard of <u>the dispensation of the grace of God</u> which is given me to you-ward:

Colossians 1:25:

25 Whereof I am made a minister, according to <u>the dispensation of God</u> which is given to me for you, to fulfil the word of God;

These verses should not be interpreted out of context but are only presented here as evidence of Paul's use of the word *dispensation*.

Many theologians have *carefully cut* or *rightly divided* the Bible into seven dispensations. It is the same as the number of days in Creation. Most critical for our purpose are two dispensations: the *Age of Law* and the *Age of Grace*. Under the Mosaic Covenant, Israel obligated itself to the keeping of the Law. The weight of which proved to be too much for them. The Gentiles, or non-Jews, were outside of this covenantal agreement. Following the Jews' rejection of their Messiah, in the last chapter of Acts, Paul makes a proclamation. Acts 28:28-29:

> 28 **Be it known therefore unto you, that the salvation of God is sent unto the Gentiles, and that they will hear it.** 29 **And when he had said these words, the Jews departed, and had great reasoning among themselves.**

The Apostle Paul wrote thirteen epistles or letters. Each letter was written to a group of believers or individuals such as Philemon, Titus, and Timothy. All of these letters, with the exception of Romans, were written to a group of people Paul knew personally. He had lived with many of them and taught them face to face. Therefore, most recipients of these letters had a general understanding of Paul's doctrines before receiving his letter. Romans was different. Some of those who had heard Paul teach personally had relocated to the capitol city of Rome. Many who had not personally met or heard Paul teach had become believers through the testimony of others. Romans was written to provide a foundation of Paul's doctrine upon which all his other letters are written. It is a comprehensive summary of Pauline doctrine and, therefore, it is placed first in the series of his epistles.

I like to use this as an example. Think about a multi-part series of some epic story. How difficult it would be to understand the full extent of a story by starting in season three? For this reason, let us consider the basis of the unique gospel message Paul preached. We must not confuse or combine his distinct message of the *Gospel of Grace* with the message of the other twelve apostles. He made three missionary trips to proclaim his gospel. The final trip was to Rome where he would be executed. Many of his later letters were written while he was a prisoner in Rome awaiting his trial.

The Apostle Paul preached a unique gospel message which Scripture tells us he personally received from the Risen Savior. This information he received was a mystery and had never been disclosed to anyone until it was disclosed to him. We will see that this gospel message was specifically directed to

Gentiles. In fact, Scripture states it very clearly. Consider the evidence recorded of his confrontation with the Risen Savior on the Road to Damascus. Acts 9:3-9:

> 3 And as he journeyed, he came near Damascus: and suddenly there shined round about him a light from heaven:
> 4 And he fell to the earth, and heard a voice saying unto him, Saul, Saul, why persecutest thou me?
>
> 5 And he said, Who art thou, Lord? And the Lord said, I am Jesus whom thou persecutest: it is hard for thee to kick against the pricks. 6 And he trembling and astonished said, Lord, what wilt thou have me to do? And the Lord said unto him, Arise, and go into the city, and it shall be told thee what thou must do.
>
> 7 And the men which journeyed with him stood speechless, hearing a voice, but seeing no man. 8 And Saul arose from the earth; and when his eyes were opened, he saw no man: but they led him by the hand, and brought him into Damascus.

9 And he was three days without sight, and neither did eat nor drink.

It is important for you to know that the Apostle Paul had never met Jesus during His earthly ministry. Therefore, he was not able to fulfill the requirements for the replacement of Judas as the twelfth apostle. (*cf.* Acts 1:21-26.)

God directs a faithful disciple named Ananias to heal Paul's blindness. Pay close attention to this dialogue between God and Ananias. Acts 9:10-16:

10 And there was a certain disciple at Damascus, named Ananias; and to him said the Lord in a vision, Ananias. And he said, Behold, I am here, Lord. 11 And the Lord said unto him, Arise, and go into the street which is called Straight, and enquire in the house of Judas for one called Saul, of Tarsus: for, behold, he prayeth, 12 And hath seen in a vision a man named Ananias coming in, and putting his hand on him, that he might receive his sight.

13 Then Ananias answered, Lord, I have heard by many of this man, how much evil he hath done to thy saints at Jeru-

salem: 14 And here he hath authority from the chief priests to bind all that call on thy name.

15 But the Lord said unto him, <u>Go thy way: for he is a chosen vessel unto me, to bear my name before the Gentiles, and kings, and the children of Israel:</u> 16 <u>For I will shew him how great things he must suffer for my name's sake.</u>

In Paul's letter to the Galatians, he writes something he most likely shared with other believers in person. These verses below recall his second meeting with the other apostles in Jerusalem. Paul had only met Peter and James once before on his previous trip. Galatians 2:1-9:

1 Then fourteen years after I went up again to Jerusalem with Barnabas, and took Titus with me also. 2 And I went up by revelation, and communicated unto them that gospel which I preach among the Gentiles, but privately to them which were of reputation, lest [for fear that] by any means I should run, or had run, in vain.

3 But neither Titus, who was with me,

being a Greek, was compelled to be circumcised: 4 And that because of false brethren unawares brought in, who came in privily to spy out our liberty which we have in Christ Jesus, that they might bring us into bondage: 5 To whom we gave place by subjection, no, not for an hour; that the truth of the gospel might continue with you.

6 But of these who seemed to be somewhat [of importance], (whatsoever they were, it maketh no matter to me: God accepteth no man's person:) for they who seemed to be somewhat in conference added nothing to me:

7 But contrariwise, when they saw that the gospel of the uncircumcision was committed unto me, as the gospel of the circumcision was unto Peter; 8 (For he that wrought effectually in Peter to the apostleship of the circumcision, the same was mighty in me toward the Gentiles:) 9 And when James, Cephas, and John, who seemed to be pillars, perceived the grace that was given unto me, they gave to me and Barnabas the right hands of fellowship; that we should go

unto the heathen, and they unto the circumcision.

Paul provides a concise statement of this gospel in a letter to the Corinthians. Notice his use of the definite article *the* when referring to *the* gospel *wherein ye stand*. This is the basis of their salvation. 1 Corinthians 15:1-4:

> 1 **Moreover, brethren, I declare unto you the gospel which I preached unto you, which also ye have received, and wherein ye stand; 2 By which also ye are saved, if ye keep in memory what I preached unto you, unless ye have believed in vain.**
>
> 3 **For I delivered unto you first of all that which I also received, [1] how that Christ died for our sins according to the scriptures; 4 [2] And that he was buried, and [3] that he rose again the third day according to the scriptures:**

We can see the simplicity of the Gospel of Grace. This gospel consists of Christ's death on the Cross, His burial, and His resurrection. It is the believing of these facts that are the basis for our salvation! Jesus Christ accomplished it all.

The sufficiency of Christ's completed work on the Cross and that nothing else can be added is made clear by Paul. This is perhaps one of the most quoted verses. Ephesians 2:8-9:

> 8 **For by grace are ye saved through faith**; and that not of yourselves: it is the gift of God: 9 **Not of works**, lest [for fear that] any man should boast.

In his letter to the Galatians, he chastised some of the believers there. They were adding works as a requirement for salvation in addition to what the Savior had already done. Today, many Christians are still adding to the simplicity of salvation by grace through faith! Paul warned the Colossians. Colossians 2:8:

> 8 **Beware lest any man spoil you through <u>philosophy</u> and <u>vain deceit</u>, after the <u>tradition of men</u>, after the <u>rudiments of the world</u>, and not after Christ.**

Paul's gospel message is different from that of the Twelve. In Galatians, he affirms that he did not receive it from the other apostles or from any other man. Furthermore, he asserts he received it directly from the Risen Savior. Galatians 1:11-12:

11 But I certify you, brethren, that the gospel which was preached of [from] me is not after [from] man.

12 For <u>I neither received it of man, neither was I taught it, but by the revelation of Jesus Christ.</u>

Years ago when I was growing up, I asked my Methodist pastor why he did not preach from Paul's letters. He told me that it was because Paul had persecuted the Church and, therefore, he rejected him. Another pastor told me that Paul's writings were only his opinion and therefore not reliable. Friend, either Scripture is inspired, infallible, and complete or it is not. The Bible is our only source of truth. It is authoritative. We have God's Word on it.

Here is Paul's view on this. Verses 13-17:

13 For ye have heard of my conversation [manner of living] in time past in the Jews' religion, how that beyond measure I persecuted the church of God, and wasted it: **14** And profited in the Jews' religion above many my equals in mine own nation, being more exceedingly zealous of the traditions of my fathers.

15 **But <u>when it pleased God</u>, who separated me from my mother's womb, and
called me by his grace,** 16 **<u>To reveal his
Son in [to] me</u>, <u>that I might preach him
among the heathen</u> [Gentiles]; immediately <u>I conferred not with flesh and
blood</u> [any man]:**

17 **<u>Neither went I up to Jerusalem to
them which were apostles before me</u>;
but [instead] I went into Arabia, and
[later] returned again unto Damascus.**

God set Paul apart for a special ministry to the
Gentiles. This did not mean that the offer of the Gospel of Grace was not also open to the Jews. It is avail-
able to everyone but effective for only those who believe. Paul continually refers to *faith* or *the act of believing* throughout his epistles.

Here is something that will help those new to
this concept that Paul is different from the other
twelve apostles. Find a large jumbo paper clip. Beginning with the last page of Acts and ending with
the first page of Hebrews place the paper clip over
the pages in between. The books contained within
the paper clip should start with Romans and end
with Philemon. These are the thirteen epistles written by Paul. All this will make sense in a moment.

In the last chapter of Acts, immediately before Paul's first book, there is a meeting recorded. It happened while Paul was incarcerated in Rome. He called the local Jewish leaders to meet with him. (*cf.* Acts 28:16-30.) After reasoning with them at great length, they left debating amongst themselves. At this point, Paul makes a declaration which is recorded in Acts 28:28:

28 Be it known therefore unto you, that <u>the salvation of God is sent unto the Gentiles,</u> and <u>that they will hear it.</u>

These are the words which end the portion of Scripture which precedes Paul's epistles. Now, let us look at the other side. If you turn to the portion of Scripture which follows Paul's epistles, the first book you come to is Hebrews. Are you starting to see a pattern here? This book is written to Jewish believers–those following *the Gospel of the Kingdom!*

The message Paul received from the Lord Jesus Christ is directed to the Gentiles. It is called the Gospel of Grace for a reason. *Grace* means *gift* and *faith* means *believing what God said.* Therefore, salvation from this gospel message comes from believing in what God has already done for you through His Son's death, burial, and resurrection. He is graciously offering salvation as a gift to anyone who will believe. Here is the best news: Christ paid the price in full!

Again, it is critical for our purpose to know about two dispensations: the *Age of Law* and the *Age of Grace*. Most pastors and teachers of the Bible believe that these two dispensations are sequential meaning that one follows the other. This is not true. The remainder of this introduction will explain why. The *Age of Law* started with Moses and was still in effect at the time of Jesus' ministry. Matthew 5:17

> 17 **Think not that I am come to destroy the law, or the prophets: I am not come to destroy, but to fulfil.**

Paul's message was about grace. He wrote in Galatians 2:21:

> 21 **I do not frustrate the grace of God: for if righteousness come by the law, then Christ is dead in vain.**

The *Age of Law* was temporarily suspended but it will resume at the close of the *Age of Grace*. It is referred to as a parenthetical interruption. The prophetic program given in Daniel 9 is in abeyance until this present age is completed. The *Age of Grace* begins with the conversion of Paul who was the first to be saved by grace through faith. It ends with the Rapture which is *His Calling* of those saved by grace through faith.

GraceWord Publishing has excellent books which explain this division in greater detail. As I mentioned before, the book entitled *Letters to Theophilus* is a summary of the entire Bible from Genesis to Revelation. On the other side of the coin, *The Glorious Destiny Of Israel* presents the promises and prophecies given to Israel.

Now, with this summary of the Age of Grace and Paul's unique gospel message outlined, we are ready to begin our study of 1 & 2 Thessalonians.

xxx

1

About Thessalonica

The Acts of the Apostles provides a record of the missionary trips of Paul. Prior to his arriving in Thessalonica, he was in Philippi where he was arrested and beaten without a trial. While he was shackled inside the inner dungeon, there was an earthquake and the prisoners were freed. You can read about this in Acts 16. Later, when the magistrates learned they had beaten and imprisoned Roman citizens, they let them loose and begged them to leave their city. Acts 16:40:

> 40 **And they went out of the prison, and entered into the house of Lydia: and when they had seen the brethren, they comforted them, and departed.**

Paul's journeys are recorded by Luke who often accompanied him. Following his departure from Philippi, Luke writes in Acts 17:1-2:

> 1 Now when they had passed through Amphipolis and Apollonia, they came to Thessalonica, where was a synagogue of the Jews: 2 And Paul, as his manner was, went in unto them, and three sabbath days reasoned with them out of the scriptures,

During the earlier part of his ministry, Paul would go to the synagogue to reason with the Jews. Romans 1:16:

> 16 For I am not ashamed of the gospel of Christ: for it is the power of God unto salvation to every one that believeth; to the Jew first, and also to the Greek.

Going into the synagogue, he argues his points before their assembly. Acts 17:3-4:

> 3 Opening and alleging, that Christ must needs have suffered, and risen again from the dead; and that this Jesus, whom I preach unto you, is Christ.
>
> 4 And some of them believed, and con-

sorted with Paul and Silas; and of the
devout Greeks a great multitude, and of
the chief women not a few.

This popular acceptance of Paul resulted in a back-
lash from some of the Jews. We will see that wher-
ever Paul would go, the pious Jews would be in constant opposition to him and his message. Verses 5-6:

5 But the Jews which [who] believed
not, moved with envy, took unto them
certain lewd fellows of the baser sort,
and gathered a company, and set all the
city on an uproar, and assaulted the
house of Jason, and sought to bring
them out to the people.

6 And when they found them not, they
drew Jason and certain brethren unto
the rulers of the city, crying, These that
have turned the world upside down are
come hither also;

The Jews gathered unto themselves a crowd of non-
productive people who joined the mob out of curios-
ity and excitement. Just as it was in Ephesus and Philippi, it now was in Thessalonica.

Charges were brought forth with accusations

that these men *all do contrary to the decrees of Caesar, saying that there is another king.* Hearing this, the magistrates were greatly troubled for fear of the emperor. Verses 7-9:

> 7 **Whom Jason hath received: and these all do contrary to the decrees of Caesar, saying that there is another king, one Jesus.** 8 **And they troubled the people and the rulers of the city, when they heard these things.** 9 **And when they had taken security of Jason, and of the other [others], they let them go.**

For his safety, the brethren thought it best if Paul continue his journey. If we use the words *three sabbath days reasoned with them* in verse 2, we can estimate the period of time to be about three weeks. This concluded Paul's brief visit with those in Thessalonica. Verses 10-11:

> 10 **And the brethren immediately sent away Paul and Silas by night unto Berea: who coming thither went into the synagogue of the Jews.** 11 **These were more noble than those in Thessalonica, in that they received the word with all readiness of mind, and searched the scriptures daily, whether those things**

were so.

This is an example of a problem that still exists today. People remain committed to what they have been taught without considering words recorded in the Bible. Like Jesus Who taught during His earthly ministry, the Pharisees rejected His teaching. Why? It conflicted with what they had been taught and believed. There is an important point being made here!

A comparison is made with those from Berea who were more noble or honorable. Why is that? Unlike the others, the Bereans listened with an open mind and then searched the Scripture to verify what Paul was saying was true. What was the result of this? Verse 12:

> 12 **Therefore many of them believed; also of honourable women which were Greeks, and of men, not a few.**

Yet, the opposition continued. Verses 13-14:

> 13 **But when the Jews of Thessalonica had knowledge that the word of God was preached of Paul at Berea, they came thither also, and stirred up the people.**

14 And then immediately the brethren sent away Paul to go as it were to the sea: but Silas and Timotheus abode there still.

Timothy and Silas remained in Berea to continue their teaching until they were called by Paul. Verse 15:

15 And they that conducted Paul brought him unto Athens: and receiving a commandment unto Silas and Timotheus for to come to him with all speed, they departed.

Such were the circumstances which surrounded Paul's first visit to Thessalonica. These two letters we are now studying were written to the grace believers established there.

2

1 Thessalonians 1

In his greeting, Paul begins by listing those who share in the ministry, Timothy and Silvanus. Some believe that these men should be considered co-authors of this letter, but the authorship belongs to the Apostle Paul alone. He includes the tokens of the Gospel of Grace which he received from the Risen Savior. These tokens or symbols are the words *grace*, extended to all men, and *peace* with God Who withholds His judgment during this *Age of Grace*. 1 Thessalonians 1:1:

> 1 **Paul, and Silvanus, and Timotheus, unto the church of the Thessalonians which is in God the Father and in the Lord Jesus Christ: Grace be unto you, and peace, from God our Father, and the Lord Jesus Christ.**

Prayers and supplications, or requests, must also include thanksgiving. He does this in his salutation. Verses 2-3:

> **2 We give thanks to God always for you all, making mention of you in our prayers; 3 Remembering without ceasing your work of faith, and labour of love, and patience of hope in our Lord Jesus Christ, in the sight of God and our Father;**

The believers, with the help of Timothy and Silas, had remained faithful to the Gospel of Grace. Evidence of this was displayed in their daily living before both God and men. Below, he writes *your election of God*. This may refer to *their choice* to choose God by their free will and accept the gospel they heard from Paul. It may also refer to those who, by believing, were sealed by the Holy Spirit and placed *in Christ* as God's elect. With this they had received God's assurance of salvation–eternal security *in Christ*. (*cf.* Eph. 2:13-14.) Verses 4-5:

> **4 Knowing, brethren beloved, your election of God.**

> **5 For our gospel came not unto you in word only, but also in power, and in the**

Holy Ghost, and in much assurance; as ye know what manner of men we were [while living] among you for your sake.

Paul and his company had stayed with them and they knew their manner of living while they were with them. Hearing their teaching and seeing their example, the Thessalonians believed the gospel and became followers.

There were Jews among them at that time causing great difficulty for Paul and his companions. In spite of their affliction, they received salvation and, with this, the Spirit of Promise. Verse 6:

> 6 And ye became followers of us, and of the Lord, having received the word in much affliction, with joy of the Holy Ghost:

Writing to the Ephesians, he describes this same event. Ephesians 1:13:

> 13 In whom ye also trusted, after that ye heard the word of truth, the gospel of your salvation: in whom also after that ye believed, ye were sealed with that holy Spirit of promise,

In the verse that follows, Paul explains what this *holy Spirit of promise* guaranties will happen in the future. Ephesians 1:14:

> 14 **Which is the earnest of our inheritance <u>until the redemption of the purchased possession,</u> unto the praise of his glory.**

The importance of this future event cannot be over emphasized as we continue our study of Thessalonians. The redemption, of which he speaks, is the completion or fulfillment of the purchased possession. We are *spiritually* placed *in Christ* the moment we believe. Yet our bodies remain here on earth until the completion of our redemption–our bodily *catching away* or Rapture.

He continues on how they are living examples of lives worthy of *His Calling*. 1 Thessalonians 1:7-9:

> 7 **So that ye were ensamples to all that believe in Macedonia and Achaia.**
>
> 8 **For from you sounded out the word of the Lord not only in Macedonia and Achaia, but also in every place your faith to God-ward is spread abroad; so that we need not to speak any thing.**

9 **For they themselves shew of us what manner of entering in we had unto you, and how ye turned to God from idols to serve the living and true God;**

Their reputation is well known. They had turned from idols to serving the one true God. They also have the hope of redemption as His purchased possession. Believers are bought by the blood of Christ. Their bodily redemption at *His Calling* will complete this purchase. The Holy Spirit guarantees it!

Paul hints of this in verse 10:

10 **And <u>to wait for his Son from heaven</u>, whom he raised from the dead, even Jesus, which delivered us from the wrath to come.**

We can look forward to exploring more of our *blessed hope* in the coming chapters.

3

1 Thessalonians 2

It was with great difficulty and opposition that Paul made it to Thessalonica to preach and teach them. He points out that they are aware of this since they were eyewitnesses. 1 Thessalonians 2:1-2:

> 1 For yourselves, brethren, know our entrance in unto you, that it was not in vain [without value]:
>
> 2 But even after that we had suffered before, and were shamefully entreated, as ye know, at Philippi, we were bold in our God to speak unto you the gospel of God with much contention [strife].

Paul and his company were bold and able to present them with the gospel of their salvation. Verses 3-4:

3 For our exhortation was not of deceit, nor of uncleanness, nor in guile: 4 But as we were allowed of [by] God to be put in trust with the gospel, even so we speak; not as pleasing men, but God, which trieth [tests or proves] our hearts.

The Thessalonians, realizing they were not trying to deceive them, trusted them. Paul lists the reasons they had confidence in them. Verses 5-6:

5 For neither at any time used we flattering words, as ye know, nor a cloke of covetousness; God is witness: 6 Nor of [from] men sought we glory, neither of you, nor yet of others, when we might have been burdensome, as the apostles of Christ.

Unlike many proselytizers, those trying to convert people to their way of thinking, Paul did not try to win them by flattery. They did not seek to be honored by them nor did they want to become a financial burden. Later, in his other letter to them, he writes about his desire not to be beholding to anyone. 2 Thessalonians 3:7-9:

7 For yourselves know how ye ought to follow us: for we behaved not ourselves

disorderly among you; 8 Neither did we eat any man's bread for nought [nothing]; but wrought [worked] with labour and travail night and day, that we might not be chargeable to any of you:

9 Not because we have not power, but to make ourselves an ensample [example] unto you to follow us.

Paul was known for earning his keep as a tentmaker while preaching in Galatia, Corinth, Ephesus, and Thessalonica. He describes their relationship with the Thessalonians while he was there staying amongst them. 1 Thessalonians 2:7-9:

7 But we were gentle among you, even as a nurse cherisheth her children: 8 So being affectionately desirous of you, we were willing to have imparted unto you, not the gospel of God only, but also our own souls, because ye were dear unto us.

9 For ye remember, brethren, our labour and travail: for [we were] labouring night and day, because we would not be chargeable unto any of you, we preached unto you the gospel of God.

Paul makes it clear to them that there was no *quid pro quo* created. In other words, what he offered to them was free. There was no exchange of value. Unfortunately, most churches today expect something in return whether it is membership, attendance, money, or volunteerism. Paul reminds them that, in sharing the gospel with them, nothing was owed or expected.

He calls upon their memories of his stay with them and his conversation, or manner of living. Verses 10-11:

> 10 **Ye are witnesses, and God also, how holily and justly and unblameably we behaved ourselves among you that believe:**

> 11 **As ye know how we exhorted and comforted and charged [instructed] every one of you, as a father doth his children,**

It is from this fatherly position as well as his apostleship that Paul encourages them to walk in a way that is worthy of *His Calling*. Verse 12:

> 12 **That ye would walk worthy of God, who hath called you unto his kingdom**

16

and glory.

In view of their faithfulness in receiving the Word of God and having it penetrate their lives, he thanks God. Verse 13:

> 13 For this cause also thank we God without ceasing, because, when ye received the word of God which ye heard of us, ye received it not as the word of men, but as it is in truth, the word of God, which effectually worketh also in you that believe.

For they too, like their brethren in Judaea, had suffered from local opposition. The Jews who killed their prophets and crucified their Messiah were now persecuting those who believed the Gospel of the Kingdom. Verses 14-15:

> 14 For ye, brethren, became followers of the churches of God which in Judaea are in Christ Jesus: for ye also have suffered like things of your own countrymen, even as they have of the Jews:
>
> 15 Who both killed the Lord Jesus, and their own prophets, and have persecuted us; and they please not God,

and are contrary to all men:

Furthermore, they try to prevent the Gentiles from hearing the Gospel of Grace by Paul and his fellow workers. Verse 16:

16 [These Jews also] Forbidding us to speak to the Gentiles that they might be saved, to fill up their sins alway: for the wrath is come upon them to the uttermost.

Although their time in Thessalonica was short, their affections for them remained. It is Paul's desire to see them again face to face. Verse 17:

17 But we, brethren, being taken from you for a short time in presence, not in heart, endeavoured the more abundantly to see your face with great desire.

The powers and principalities that rule this world were preventing them from returning to enjoy their fellowship. (cf. Eph. 6:12.) Verse 18:

18 Wherefore we would have come unto you, even I Paul, once and again; but Satan hindered us.

However, for the grace believer, he reminds them of the promise that brings hope and joy. Verses 19-20:

> 19 **For what is our hope, or joy, or crown of rejoicing? Are not even ye [will be] in the presence of our Lord Jesus Christ at his coming?**
>
> 20 **For ye are our glory and joy.**

What is the reason for this hope? Paul is referring to the Rapture–the *catching away* of the believers. Like them, he reminds us that we will be *in the presence of our Lord Jesus Christ at His Coming!*

4

1 Thessalonians 3

After Paul and his companions had left Thessalonica, they were busy furthering the gospel. However, his concerns for them remained unabated. It was decided that Paul would remain in Athens alone and Timothy would return to them to increase their knowledge in the faith. 1 Thessalonians 3:1-2:

1 **Wherefore when we could no longer forbear [continue], we thought it good [for me] to be left at Athens alone;**

2 **And sent Timotheus, our brother, and minister of God, and our fellow-labourer in the gospel of Christ, to establish you, and to comfort you concerning your faith:**

Paul wants the Thessalonians to be firmly established in the truth of the gospel and the Word of God.

Affliction will come and is inevitable in view of their faith. Having both their feet firmly planted on the Word of God, they will be able to stand. Verse 3:

> 3 **That no man should be moved by these afflictions: for yourselves know that we are appointed thereunto.**

They saw what Paul went through while he was with them. He warns them that they too will suffer afflictions and tribulation. All who follow Christ will suffer like Him. Verses 4:

> 4 **For verily, when we were with you, we told you before that we should suffer tribulation; even as it came to pass, and ye know.**

This is a common theme in Paul's letters. He writes about the sufferings and troubles of those in Corinth. 2 Corinthians 1:3-7:

> 3 **Blessed be God, even the Father of our Lord Jesus Christ, the Father of mercies, and the God of all comfort; 4 Who comforteth us in all our tribulation, that we may be able to comfort them which are**

in any trouble, by the comfort wherewith we ourselves are comforted of
God.

5 For as the sufferings of Christ abound
in us, so our consolation also aboundeth by Christ. 6 And whether we be af-
flicted, it is for your consolation and
salvation, which is effectual in the en-
during of the same sufferings which we
also suffer: or whether we be comforted, it is for your consolation and salvation.

7 And our hope of you is stedfast, knowing, that as ye are partakers of the sufferings, so shall ye be also of the consolation.

The word *consolation* means *the act of comforting.* It is
interesting that the Lord Jesus Christ refers to the the
Holy Spirit as *The Comforter.* (*cf.* Jn. 14:26.) Being comforted by the Holy Spirit, they are to comfort others.

Paul was concerned that Satan and his angels
would beguile those who believed the Gospel of
Grace. This would make his investment in their
learning vain or of no value. 1 Thessalonians 3:5:

5 For this cause, when I could no longer forbear [continue], I sent to know your faith, lest by some means the tempter have tempted you, and our labour [work in you] be in vain.

Timothy returned from Thessalonica and brought favorable news that comforted Paul. Verse 6:

6 But now when Timotheus came from you unto us, and brought us good tidings of your faith and charity, and that ye have good remembrance [memories] of us always, desiring greatly to see us, as we also [desire] to see you:

Both parties desired to see and comfort each other in fellowship again.

Learning of their steadfastness in the faith was, in itself, a comfort to Paul during his own afflictions. Verses 7-9:

7 Therefore, brethren, we were comforted over you in all our affliction and distress by your faith:

8 For now we live, if ye stand fast in the Lord.

9 **For what thanks can we render to God again for you, for all the joy wherewith we joy for your sakes before our God;**

In spite of his troubles, Paul had a wonderful prayer life with his Savior. He was in constant communication with Him regarding everything. He prayed for his needs and concerns, but he always included thanksgiving. His prayers are excellent examples as to how believers should pray. Verse 10:

10 **Night and day praying exceedingly that we might see your face, and might perfect that which is lacking in your faith.**

Paul wants to return to the believers in Thessalonica to see them again and strengthen their faith. He wants them to increase in their love–the fruit of their faith. Verses 11-12:

11 **Now God himself and our Father, and our Lord Jesus Christ, direct our way unto you.**

12 **And the Lord make you to increase and abound in love one toward another, and toward all men, even as we do toward you:**

To fully understand the importance of love in the lives of believers and its relationship to tribulation, let us look at two verses from Paul. The first is Romans 5:3-5:

> **3 And not only so, but we glory in tribulations also: knowing that tribulation worketh patience; 4 And patience, experience; and experience, hope:**

> **5 And hope maketh not ashamed; because <u>the love of God is shed abroad in our hearts</u> by the Holy Ghost which is given unto us.**

This love which fills and overflows in our hearts is the outpouring of God's love by the Holy Spirit.

Throughout all the turmoil in our lives, we have one constant upon which we can confidently stand. Nothing can separate us from the love of God which, for grace believers, is in Christ Jesus! Look at Romans 8:38-39:

> **38 For I am persuaded, that neither death, nor life, nor angels, nor principalities, nor powers, nor things present, nor things to come,**

39 Nor height, nor depth, nor any other creature, shall be able to separate us from the love of God, which is in Christ Jesus our Lord.

He concludes with this thought. Believers are to be blameless in the lives they lead. The word *holy* means *separated from the world*. 1 Thessalonians 3:13:

13 To the end <u>he may stablish your hearts unblameable in holiness before God</u>, even our Father, <u>at the coming of our Lord Jesus Christ with all his saints.</u>

There are two ways in which the last line can be interpreted. If we are confident in our system of interpretation, we would not consider this to refer to His Second Coming with His saints. At that point, He is coming to do battle with the nations of the world in defence of Israel.

At the end of each of the last three chapters Paul refers to *His Calling*. The answer will be revealed in the next chapter where we will read in 1 Thessalonians 4:17:

17 Then we which are alive and remain shall be caught up together with them in the clouds, to meet the Lord in the air:

and so shall we ever be with the Lord.

Reading the above verse, we learn that when we are *caught up together* in the clouds. My friend, this is *the Rapture*. From that point in time, we will be forever with Christ. 1 Thessalonians 3:12:

> 12 **And the Lord make you to increase and abound in love one toward another, and toward all men, even as we do toward you:**

Being made to abound in love towards one another and all men will produce the desired result in the end. Verse 13 begins with these same words *to the end*. This means *the end result* or *the ultimate purpose*. Ephesians tells us that when we are saved, we are spiritually placed *in Christ*.

> 13 **To the end [that] he may [1] stablish your hearts unblameable in holiness [when we are presented] before God, even our Father, at the coming of our Lord Jesus Christ with all his saints.**

We are also told that those saved by grace through faith will be conformed to the image of His Son. (*cf.* Rom. 8:29.) Therefore, in the end, Christ will present Himself before God the Father in His righteousness.

He will also present all the saints before God. These are the one who have been secure *in Him* since they believed the Gospel of Grace. They have been conformed to His image and are like Him – holy and blameless. When will this be? It will be at *His Calling!*

5

1 Thessalonians 4

Paul furthers desires that these believers abound with love towards each other as well as towards all men. He continues by *beseeching,* or imploring, and *exhorting* them. His words are intended to incite them to action and encourage them. Verses 4:1-2:

> 1 **Furthermore then we beseech you, brethren, and exhort you by the Lord Jesus, that as ye have received of us how ye ought to walk and to please God, so ye would abound more and more. 2 For ye know what commandments we gave you by the Lord Jesus.**

In this last verse, Paul uses the word *commandments*

which means *instruction* but with apostolic authority. It would be contrary to Paul's teaching to add keeping any part of the Law as a requirement for salvation by grace. (*cf.* Rom. 11:6.)

He writes about the moral and ethical expectations of those saved by grace. They must put off sexual desires which defile their bodies. Verses 3-5:

> 3 **For this is the will of God, even [that is to say] your sanctification, that ye should abstain from fornication:**
>
> 4 **That every one of you should know how to possess his vessel [body] in sanctification and honour;**
>
> 5 **Not in the lust of concupiscence [strong sexual desire], even [that is to say] as the Gentiles which know not God:**

There is a high standard of care concerning how believers are to interact with each other. Verse 6:

> 6 **That no man go beyond and defraud his brother in any matter: because that the Lord is the avenger of all such, as we**

also have forewarned you and testified.

As believers, we are called to be separated from the world and its uncleanness. Paul returns to abounding in love towards each other and all men by making the following statement. He tells us that whoever despises or has contempt is not despising other men, but instead is despising God. Consider how angry we can be with *other people*. Then, realize that we are actually despising God Who made them. Verses 7-8:

> 7 **For God hath not called us unto uncleanness, but unto holiness. 8 He therefore that despiseth, despiseth not man, but God, who hath also given unto us his holy Spirit.**

This makes me think about the private conversations I have with other drivers when I am behind the wheel. All of us are sinners and it is our day-to-day activities about which Paul wants us to think. It is easier to love those who are also saved than those who are enemies with God. When I think about unsaved people, it helps me to ask a question. When I am angry at someone, I ask myself, "Didn't Christ also die for them?"

Paul returns to addressing this love that the

Thessalonians share with each other. Verse 9:

> 9 **But as touching brotherly love ye need not that I write unto you: for ye yourselves are taught of God to love one another.**

When it comes to brotherly love, they have this down. Not only is their love known within their own fellowship, but also throughout the region of Macedonia. He asks that they continue to grow this love. Verse 10:

> 10 **And indeed ye do it toward all the brethren which are in all Macedonia: but we beseech you, brethren, that ye increase more and more;**

Concerning their *manner of living*, Paul writes they should lead quiet and peaceful lives before all men. This is done by diligently going about their own affairs and walking honorably among those who are not saved. Verse 11:

> 11 **And that ye study to be quiet, and to do your own business, and to work with your own hands, as we commanded you;**

He speaks of those who are not saved as being out-side the assembly or being *without*. Verse 12:

> 12 **That ye may walk honestly toward them that are without, and that ye may have lack of nothing.**

The Thessalonians were concerned about those who had preceded them in death. They had loved ones and fellow believers who had died. What was going to happen to them? Paul alleviates their concern. Verse 13:

> 13 **But I would not have you to be igno-rant, brethren, concerning them which are asleep, that ye sorrow not, even as others which have no hope.**

He refers to those who had already died as being asleep. He is referring to their body, since, spiritu-ally, all believers are *in Christ* Who is seated at the right hand of the Father. He tells them not to sorrow like unbelievers who are without hope. Verse 14:

> 14 **For if we believe that Jesus died and rose again, even so them also which sleep in Jesus will God bring with him.**

We know that the gospel of our salvation is Christ's

death, His burial, and His resurrection. Paul assures them that His promise still stands. Those believers who die before the Rapture are asleep in Christ. They will appear before God *with Christ* at *His Calling*.

The resurrection of the body must be seen as the completion of our redemption. At the moment of our salvation, we are saved. We receive the Holy Spirit Who is the presence of God within us. We are spiritually placed *in Christ* Who is seated in heaven. King David wrote about what is happening right now in Psalms 110:1:

> **1 The LORD [GOD] said unto my Lord,**
> **Sit thou at my right hand, until I make**
> **thine enemies thy footstool.**

Prior to the seven-year Tribulation, Christ will call His own to Himself.

Paul tells the Thessalonians who will participate in this great day–the day or *His Calling*. The word *prevent* means *to precede* or *to go before*. He certifies this is the Word of the Lord. 1 Thessalonians 4:15:

> **15 For this we say unto you by the word**
> **of the Lord, that <u>we which are alive</u> <u>and</u>**
> **<u>remain unto the coming of the Lord</u>**

shall not prevent them which [who] are asleep.

He is creating an order of this event. Those who are still alive at the time of *His Calling*, will not go first. He continues with verse 16:

16 **For the Lord himself shall descend from heaven with a shout, with the voice of the archangel, and with the trump of God: and the dead in Christ shall rise first:**

We must not assume this means He will fully descend for He remains in the air as we will see from the text. Those who are asleep *in Christ* will have their bodies raised first; then, those who are alive, will join them *in the air*. Verse 17:

17 **Then we which are alive and remain shall be caught up together with them in the clouds, to meet the Lord in the air: and so shall we ever be with the Lord.**

We will be caught up together in the clouds. We will meet the Lord Jesus Christ in the air. This event is separate from His *Second Coming* when He returns to rescue Israel. This *catching away* or *Rapture* is the completion of our redemption. Thereafter, we will be forever *with Him!*

Let us just stop for a moment and think about this. When we come to the realization of what is going to happen to us, we should comfort fellow believers with our blessed hope. Verse 18:

> 18 **Wherefore comfort one another with these words.**

How can we be sure this will happen? It is simple. We have God's Word on it!

6

1 Thessalonians 5

The Rapture or "catching away" of His believers is imminent. There is no event which must precede it. However, this is not true for the *Second Coming* which follows the seven-year Tribulation. The time of the Rapture is unknown. It is the cause There is a temporary suspension of the Age of Law in effect. This is explained by Paul in Romans 11:25:

> **25 For I would not, brethren, that ye should be ignorant of this mystery, lest ye should be wise in your own conceits; <u>that blindness in part is happened to Israel, until the fulness of the Gentiles be come in.</u>**

Therefore, something is going on with the Gentiles and until that is completed, the Prophetic Program dealing with Israel will be, again, temporarily suspended. When the fullness of the Gentiles during this Age of Grace is complete, the Age of Law will resume. God does not disclose the exact time as it would be contrary to His purposes. Until then, we are to remain faithful and look for *His Calling*.

When Jesus sat with His disciples after His resurrection, they asked Him a question. Pay attention to His response. Acts 1:6-7:

> 6 **When they therefore were come together, they asked of him, saying, Lord, wilt thou at this time restore again the kingdom to Israel?**
>
> 7 **And he said unto them, <u>It is not for you to know the times or the seasons, which the Father hath put in his own power.</u>**

The book *Letters To Theophilus–Are You Ready For The End Times* is published by GraceWord. It goes into a full explanation of the seven dispensations. The *Second Coming* is Jesus' return to save Israel from the godless nations. This will happen at the end of Daniel's 70th Week which is known as Jacob's Time of Testing or The Tribulation. Since it occurs at the end of this week, what will start this week of seven years? It is the Rapture. Here is an important point. Again, the *Second Coming* is not imminent. It can only come at the fulfillment of Daniel's prophecy. *Imminent* means it can happen at any time. The Rapture, to the joy of all grace believers, is *imminent!*

The Thessalonians are aware of the coming Rapture which Paul refers to as *the Day of the Lord.* Verses 1 Thessalonians 5:1-2:

> 1 **But of the times and the seasons, brethren, ye have no need that I write unto you.** 2 **For yourselves know perfectly that the day of the Lord so cometh as a thief in the night.**

Speaking of the unsaved, Paul writes in verse 3:

> 3 **For when they shall say, Peace and safety; then sudden destruction cometh upon them, as travail upon a woman with child; and they shall not escape.**

With the Rapture, the Tribulation begins. For those who remain on earth, there is no escape.

Paul now writes about those saved by grace. Verses 4-5:

> 4 **But ye, brethren, are not in darkness**

[unknown], that that day should over-take you as a thief.

5 Ye are all the children of light, and the children of the day: we are not of the night, nor of darkness.

Being children of light, he urges them to be vigilant and not in a stupor as one who is asleep. Be awake! Be sober! They are to remain separate from those who practice their deeds in the darkness. Verses 6-7:

6 Therefore let us not sleep, as do others; but let us watch and be sober.

7 For they that sleep [do] sleep in the night; and they that be drunken are drunken in the night.

In Ephesians, Paul writes about the armor of God. It is defensive in its purpose. He mentions two pieces of armor. The helmet protects the head which is our thoughts. The breastplate protects the emotions of man which is his heart. He writes similarly to the Thessalonians in verse 8:

8 But let us, who are of the day, be sober, putting on the breastplate of faith and love; and for an helmet, the hope of sal-

vation.

What is the source of this protection? What protects our hearts and our minds? It is the Word of God! We must continue to renew our minds and, with that, our emotions. In many of Paul's letters he prays that the believers be filled with the *knowledge* and *wisdom* of God. (*cf.* Rom. 11:33, 1 Cor. 12:8, Eph. 1:17, Col. 1:9, 2:3.). We get this *knowledge* and *wisdom* of God from immersing ourselves in Scripture. This allows us to plant our feet firmly upon the solid ground and to withhold attacks, tribulation, afflictions, and sufferings for Christ's sake. All this is done by *knowledge* and *wisdom* of the *Word of God.*

Many people ask if they will go through the Tribulation. To get the answer, let us use the *Word of God* to put our hearts and minds at ease. What is the Tribulation? It is a time of judgment and testing. Like a refiner's fire, it will purify what is not pure. It will test the faith of those whose faith must be proven. Does this sound like those who are saved by grace, redeemed by the blood of Christ, and are eternally secure in Him? It most certainly is not! We are safe *in Christ.* It is His righteousness and not ours that saved us! His righteousness does not need to be tested by God. He has already approved it.

In the next verse, Paul uses the word *wrath*

which means *furious anger, intense exasperation* or *righteous indignation*. Is this to be directed at God's Son? As you read this, dear believer, this confirms we are eternally secure in Him. Verses 9-10:

> 9 **For God <u>hath not appointed us</u> to wrath, but [instead] to obtain salvation by our Lord Jesus Christ,**
>
> 10 **Who died for us, that, whether we wake [are alive] or [our bodies] sleep, <u>we should live together with him.</u>**

So, whether our bodies are alive or dead, we have God's assurance that He will neither judge His Son nor those saved by His grace who are *in Him.*

This is wonderful news! Those who are without hope are destined for testing and judgment. However, God's children, at this very moment, are secure in His Son Who will live forever. Believers need to remind each other of this glorious news. When we face afflictions and sufferings, remember these are only for a moment when compared to eternity with Him. Verse 11:

> 11 **Wherefore comfort yourselves together, and edify one another, even as also ye [already] do.**

Within every group of believers, there are individuals who are experienced and act as role models or teachers. Paul chooses the word *admonish* to describe those who labor among the believers. The word *admonish* means *to reprove with mildness, counsel, and teach.* They are not to rule over the other believers. Instead, they are to build them up; encouraging them to grow and mature *in Christ.* Verses 12-13:

12 **And we beseech you, brethren, to know them which labour among you, and are over you in the Lord, and admonish you;**

13 **And to esteem them very highly in love for their work's sake. And be at peace among yourselves.**

Here are some instructions for those in leadership regarding how they should deal with the believers. Verses 14-15:

14 **Now we exhort you, brethren, warn them that are unruly, comfort the feebleminded, support the weak, be patient toward all men.**

15 **See that none render evil for evil unto any man; but ever follow that which is**

good, both among yourselves, and to all men.

Leaders should never forget to have joy in serving the body of believers. This must be coupled with prayer and thanksgiving which is desirous of the Lord Jesus Christ. Verses 16-22:

> 16 **Rejoice evermore.** 17 **Pray without ceasing.** 18 **In every thing give thanks: for this is the will of God in Christ Jesus concerning you.**
>
> 19 **Quench not the Spirit.** 20 **Despise not prophesyings.** 21 **Prove [test] all things; hold fast that which is good.** 22 **Abstain from all appearance of evil.**

Paul begins the closing of his letter. He does this with a *benediction* or *words of blessing* to the Thessalonians. Verses 23-24:

> 23 **And <u>the very God of peace sanctify you wholly</u>; and I pray God your whole spirit and soul and body be preserved blameless unto the coming of our Lord Jesus Christ.**
>
> 24 <u>**Faithful is he that calleth you, who**</u>

also will do it.

He adds a request that they pray for the ministry of reconciliation to God which is by grace through faith in the finished work of Christ. Verse 25:

25 Brethren, pray for us.

The holy kiss is done cheek to cheek on either side of the face. Some cultures still practice this although others now reserve it for family and close friends. For members of the fellowship, it is a sign of their familial connection. Verse 26:

26 Greet all the brethren with an holy kiss.

It became a custom that all of Paul's letters be read to the local congregation and shared with others. It was a means of spreading apostolic teaching that could be applied to all believers–holy brethren. Verse 27:

27 I charge you by the Lord that this epistle be read unto all the holy brethren.

He closes with this statement. The grace of the Lord Jesus Christ, Who is the great I AM, Who was, and is, and is to come be with them always. Verse 28:

28 The grace of our Lord Jesus Christ be with you. Amen.

His last words in this letter remind the readers that the grace received by God through His Son remains forever.

7

2 Thessalonians 1

Paul writes another letter to the Thessalonians. He begins by naming those who are with him. Due to his problem with sight, he dictates his letters to a scribe. Those who are with him may listen and discuss its contents, but its authorship is attributed to the Apostle Paul. Verse 1:

> 1 **Paul, and Silvanus, and Timotheus, unto the church of the Thessalonians in God our Father and the Lord Jesus Christ:**

He adds a greeting which is specific to the Gospel of Grace. It acknowledges God's gracious offer of amnesty to all during this Age of Grace and, through it, peace with God through His Son. Verse 2:

2 Grace unto you, and peace, from God our Father and the Lord Jesus Christ.

The Thessalonians were familiar with Paul and his teaching. He lived with them and Timothy continued to help them grow *in Christ*. In his second letter, Paul expresses his gratitude to God for them. Verses 3-4:

3 We are bound to thank God always for you, brethren, as it is meet [suitable], because that your faith groweth exceedingly, and the charity [love] of every one of you all toward each other aboundeth;

4 So that we ourselves glory in you in the churches of God for your patience and faith in all your persecutions and tribulations that ye endure:

They showed patience and faith to everyone in spite of their sufferings and trials.

He gives the credit to God for abundant proof of their faith. This yield of spiritual fruit does not come from the individual but comes from the Spirit within. Therefore, it is the Spirit Who produces the evidence of their worthiness. Verse 5:

5 Which is a manifest token [evident sign] of the righteous judgment [approval] of God, that ye may be counted worthy of the kingdom of God, for which ye also suffer:

While we remain on earth in our bodies, these two will coexist: righteousness and suffering. To the believers at Philippi, Paul also writes about this. Philippians 3:9-10:

9 And [that I] be found in him, <u>not having mine own righteousness</u>, which is of the law, <u>but that which is through the faith of Christ</u>, <u>the righteousness which is of God by faith</u>:

10 That I may know him, and the power of his resurrection, and <u>the fellowship of his sufferings</u>, <u>being made conformable unto his death;</u>

We are sojourners on earth awaiting *His Calling*. As we wait, we will suffer as Christ did and, through this, be conformed into His likeness. Through the sufferings of believers, God is forming us into the image of His glorious Son. Friend, we must see this as being something good, something beneficial to us! Romans 8:28-29:

28 And we know that all things work together for good to them that love God, to them who are the called according to his purpose.

29 For whom he did foreknow, he also did predestinate to be conformed to the image of his Son, that he might be the firstborn among many brethren.

We must know that these sufferings are from Satan. How is the believer to react towards individuals who cause them pain and anguish? We return to 2 Thessalonians 1:6-9:

6 Seeing it is a righteous thing with God to recompense [repay] tribulation to them that trouble you; 7 And to you who are troubled rest with us [*in Christ*], when the Lord Jesus shall be revealed from heaven with his mighty angels,

8 In flaming fire taking vengeance on them that know not God, and that obey not the gospel of our Lord Jesus Christ: 9 Who shall be punished with everlasting destruction from the presence of the Lord, and from the glory of his power;

Similarly, in Romans, Paul writes to them about their sufferings. Romans 12:17-21:

> 17 **Recompense [repay] to no man evil for evil. Provide things honest in the sight of all men.** 18 **If it be possible, as much as lieth in you, live peaceably with all men.**
>
> 19 **Dearly beloved, <u>avenge not yourselves</u>, but rather give place unto wrath: for it is written, <u>Vengeance is mine; I will repay</u>, saith the Lord.**
>
> 20 **Therefore if thine enemy hunger, feed him; if he thirst, give him drink: for in so doing thou shalt heap coals of fire on his head.**
>
> 21 **Be not overcome of [by] evil, but overcome evil with good.**

These words are written to all who believe in God and accept His Gospel of Grace. 2 Thessalonians 2:10:

> 10 **When he shall come to be glorified in his saints, and to be admired in all them that believe (because our testimony**

among you was believed) in that day.

In this case, the end justifies His means. We share in His pain and suffering which will bring us to the Rapture. We are being made like Him–conformed to the image of His Son. And, in the end, we too will share in His glory with Him. This will be the completion of our redemption guaranteed by the holy Spirit of Promise. (*cf.* Eph. 1:14.)

Presently, God continues to work within all believers. There is a process He begins in every believer the moment they are saved. When they believe the gospel of their salvation, they are justified by God and sealed by the holy Spirit of Promise. (*cf.* Eph. 1:13.) They are declared *not guilty* and are no longer worthy of punishment. All of their past, present, and future sins have been forgiven. The new believer receives *the righteousness of Christ*. Spiritually, they are *in Christ*. Through their afflictions and sufferings they will be conformed into Christ's death. In the end, *He will be glorified in us*.

This process by which we are conformed into His image is called *sanctification*. It is this process, while on earth, believers are made *holy* which means *being separated to God and from the world*. This process sounds daunting and most believers struggle with it.

However, it must be seen from a different perspective. It must be seen not from our perspective but from God's perspective!

Many Christians feel they must *work* in order to earn their salvation. This is wrong. God has already done the *work* necessary for our salvation. Similarly, many Christians feel they must *work* to be sanctified. Friends, this too, I believe is wrong. In the believer's life, it is always, repeat always, about Christ. Look at what Paul writes to the believers in Philippi and consider the words. Philippians 1:6:

> 6 **Being confident of this very thing, <u>that he which hath begun a good work</u> in you <u>[He] will perform it</u> until the day of Jesus Christ:**

He is telling us that we can be confident of this. It is not about us! It is about Christ! Therefore, it is not about us sanctifying ourselves, but Christ in us Who is now completing the process which He Himself started. Friend, we all need to stop and take a moment to think about this. Our sins have been forgiven. We are to abstain from worldly lusts and sin. We are to rejoice. We are to be filled with joy!

I was attending my adult daughter's baptism and heard this from the pulpit of a conservative Baptist church. "We all know that we are saved by grace through faith without works." There was a resounding sound of amens. Then, the pastor continued, "But, we also know that we must continue to do good works to keep our salvation." This is so wrong. It is completely contrary to the Gospel of Grace. Every need for our salvation was accomplished through Christ's finished work . . . period!

In like manner, we must exercise our faith in Christ during our sanctification. We must be confident of what we have been taught. During this time, know this: He is doing the necessary work. This should help you to rejoice and be filled with joy. We are instructed by Paul to exercise our faith by believing in Him. We are to hold the *Word of God* in our hearts and minds. This may sound too easy for something way too difficult. In fact, some may say that this is *foolishness!* Let us look and see what Paul says about *foolishness.* In his first letter to the believers in Corinth, he used this word seven times. Let us consider them:

1 Corinthians 1:18-25:

> 18 **For the preaching of the cross is to them that perish <u>foolishness</u>; but unto us which are saved it is the power of God. 19 For it is written, I will destroy**

the wisdom of the wise, and will bring to nothing the understanding of the prudent.

20 Where is the wise? where is the scribe? where is the disputer of this world? hath not God made foolish the wisdom of this world? 21 For after that in the wisdom of God the world by wisdom knew not God, it pleased God by the foolishness of preaching to save them that believe.

22 For the Jews require a sign, and the Greeks seek after wisdom: 23 But we preach Christ crucified, unto the Jews a stumblingblock, and unto the Greeks foolishness; 24 But unto them which are called, both Jews and Greeks, Christ the power of God, and the wisdom of God.

25 Because the foolishness of God is wiser than men; and the weakness of God is stronger than men.

1 Corinthians 2:14-16:

14 But the natural man receiveth not the things of the Spirit of God: for they are

foolishness unto him: neither can he know them, because they are spiritually discerned. ¹⁵ But he that is spiritual judgeth all things, yet he himself is judged of no man. ¹⁶ For who hath known the mind of the Lord, that he may instruct him? But we have the mind of Christ.

Having *the mind of Christ* is *seeing things from His perspective.* That is only possible by studying *His Word.* Here is the last verse.

1 Corinthians 3:19-21:

> ¹⁹ For the wisdom of this world is foolishness with God. For it is written, He taketh the wise in their own craftiness. ²⁰ And again, The Lord knoweth the thoughts of the wise, that they are vain, ²¹ Therefore let no man glory in men. For all things are [already] yours;

If we are to suffer like Christ, let us consider Him as our example. Not only did He experience this, as we do today, He knew in advance this would happen. Isaiah 53:3:

> ₃ He is despised and rejected of men; a

man of sorrows, and acquainted with grief: and we hid as it were our faces from him; he was despised, and we esteemed him not.

He drew His strength from God His Father Who was in Him for they were One. Jesus Christ, the Man, knew this would happen and, like Him, we have the Spirit of God within us! Can you see this? Presently, God is working the process of sanctification in us. We must have faith that the Holy Spirit is doing the work. What we must do is live our lives in a manner worthy of *His Calling*. With this, we can return to 2 Thessalonians 1:11:

> 11 **Wherefore also we pray always for you, that our God would [(1)] count you worthy of this calling, and [(2) God would] fulfil all the good pleasure of his goodness, and the work of faith with power:**

Notice that it is God Who will consider you (1) worthy of *His Calling* and (2) having fulfilled His will by the work of faith. It is His power, not our efforts, that conform us to the image of His Son!

Spiritually, grace believers are secure *in Christ* in heaven. Here on earth as we await *His Calling*, the

Spirit of God is working *in us* to complete what He has already begun. Knowing this, how much more we should desire to glorify the Lord Jesus Christ! Verse 12:

> 12 **That <u>the name of our Lord Jesus Christ may be glorified</u> in you, and ye in him, <u>according to the grace of our God and the Lord Jesus Christ</u>.**

8

2 Thessalonians 2

Paul is writing about the Rapture using the words *the coming of our Lord Jesus Christ.* He calls it the *gathering* which is the bringing together of those who are His own. Paul calls these grace believers the Body of Christ. 1 Corinthians 12:27:

> 27 Now <u>ye are the body of Christ</u>, and members in particular.

Therefore, at *His Calling,* the Lord Jesus Christ is gathering His Body unto Himself of which He is the Head. 2 Thessalonians 2:1-2:

> 1 Now we beseech you, brethren, by <u>the coming of our Lord Jesus Christ</u>, and by <u>our gathering together unto him</u>, 2 That ye be not soon shaken in mind, or be troubled, neither by spirit, nor by word,

nor by letter as from us, as that the day of Christ is at hand.

Nothing is to trouble us or concern us. Nothing is to cause us to question what we firmly believe by faith. He continues by referring to *His Coming* for us as *the Day of Jesus Christ.* (*cf.* 1 Cor.1:8, 5:5, 2 Cor. 1:14, Phil. 1:6, 1:10, 2:16, 1 Thes 5:2, 2 Thes. 2:2.) For this is His day and God has been preparing us for it by conforming us to *the image of His Son.*

We must not confuse *His Appearing*, which is *His Calling* of believers to Himself, with His *Second Coming*. Paul is writing about the *Appearing* of the Lord Jesus Christ in the sky to call those who are saved by grace through faith unto Himself. At His Second Coming, which is a different event, He will be the eternal King returning to do battle with the nations who seek to destroy Israel.

There are many who teach contrary to this saying these two events are the same. However, let Scripture be our guide and not the words or traditions of men! Many pastors teach their followers they need to win the world to Christ so they can bring in His Kingdom. This is a complete lie. It is not about the believers accomplishing anything. It was, is, and will always be about Christ! The works of men are nothing more than their attempt to bring glory to themselves. Paul warns grace believers in Colossians 2:8:

> 8 **Beware lest any man spoil you through philosophy and vain deceit, after the tradition of men, after the rudiments of the world,** and not after Christ.

In like manner, he writes this in 2 Thessalonians 2:3:

> 3 Let no man deceive you by any means: **for that day shall not come,** except there come a falling away first, **and that man of sin be revealed,** the son of perdition;

Before *the Day of our Lord Jesus Christ* occurs, Paul tells us there will be a falling away, a turning away from the belief in God. He tells us *the son of perdition* or the *man of sin* will be revealed. Who is this *man?* It is important for us to know. The ending of the Age of Grace and resumption of the Age of Law will occur simultaneously. Let us consider the root of the word *perdition.* It comes from the Latin word meaning *utter destruction.* If this man is *the son of utter destruction,* it is easy to determine who is the *father of utter destruction.* The revealing of this *son of perdition* is the appearing of the Antichrist.

In the book *Letters To Theophilus*, I go into great detail to explain the seven dispensations as well as Daniel's prophecy. The 70th week is the last seven years known as the Tribulation. For our purpose here, I must summarize. The prophecy given to Daniel concerns the fulfillment of the promises made to Abraham and King David. It is the establishment of the eternal throne of the Seed of Abraham and the Seed of David: the Lord Jesus Christ. These seven years begin with the Antichrist making a covenant of peace allowing the Jews to return to Jerusalem, rebuild their temple, and resume their sacrifices. However, this is a deception. Its purpose is to gather the Jews together in Israel so that they can be destroyed once and for all.

Halfway through the seven years, the Antichrist breaks his covenant. He enters the temple and sits there proclaiming that he is God. Verses 4-5:

> 4 **Who opposeth [God] and exalteth himself above all that is called God, or that is worshipped; so that he [the Antichrist acting] as God sitteth in the temple of God, shewing himself that he is God.**

> 5 **Remember ye not, that, when I was yet with you, I told you these things?**

He is an impersonator of God, an imposter. What is sad is that most of the fallen world will rush to worship him. This being exactly what he desires. This is not something new for the Thessalonians. They had learned about Daniel's prophecy when Paul taught them the Scriptures rightly divided. He now reminds them of this.

Should the meaning of any verse get confusing, the only thing we can do is let Scripture interpret Scripture. A lot of people get this wrong. In the next verse, someone is being withheld and, at a future point in time, this person will be revealed. Who is it? Verse 6:

> 6 **And now ye know what [who] withholdeth that he might be revealed in his time.**

This cannot be the Antichrist! He will already have revealed himself (v. 3). Then, Who is this Someone? It is the Lord Jesus Christ Who will be revealed *in His time!* Look, again, at Psalms 110:1:

> 1 **The LORD [Elohim] said unto my Lord [Adonai], Sit thou at my right hand, until I make thine enemies thy footstool.**

At His resurrection, Jesus Christ was exalted and seated at the right hand of God the Father *until* His enemies were made His footstool. The seventieth week of Daniel must come to an end before His revelation. This man of perdition, the Antichrist, must be allowed to fully exalt himself (v. 4).

The next verse is also the subject of debate among Christians. Let us unpack it piece by piece using Scripture to define Scripture. The word *letteth,* a form of the verb *to let,* was first used in the record of Creation. Genesis 1:3:

> 3 **And God said, <u>Let there be light: and there was light.</u>**

God has the authority to allow. He can also use His authority or power to prevent or not allow. So, in the following verse, the One Who has the power to allow or not allow is God. Friend, Paul tells us there is an invisible battle going on. Ephesians 6:12

> 12 **For we wrestle not against flesh and blood, but against principalities, against powers, against the rulers of the darkness of this world, against spiritual wickedness in high places.**

These principalities, powers, and rulers of *the dark-*

ness of this world will be allowed to gain power but only so far as God *letteth* or *alloweth!*

Before their salvation, grace believers were once *children of darkness* as well. Ephesians 2:2:

> 2 **Wherein in time past ye walked according to the course of this world, <u>according to the prince of the power of the air, the spirit that now worketh in the children of disobedience</u>:**

A *mystery* is something hidden until it is revealed. Paul explains the *mystery of iniquity*. Satan, the prince of the power of the air, and his spirit are now working in the children of disobedience. They have been blinded and cannot see what we as believers can see. 2 Thessalonians 2:7:

> 7 **For the mystery of iniquity doth already work: only he [God] <u>who now letteth will let</u>, until he [the Antichrist] be taken out of the way.**

The Antichrist, who is the human manifestation of Satan, will be allowed to work *until he be taken out of the way*. Until that point, Paul tells believers what they can expect. 2 Timothy 3:13:

13 But evil men and seducers shall wax [grow] worse and worse, deceiving, and being deceived.

He continues writing about the Antichrist in verses 2 Thessalonians 2:8:

8 And then shall that Wicked [One] be revealed, whom the Lord shall consume with the spirit of his mouth, and shall destroy with the brightness of his coming:

Paul is writing about the *Second Coming* when the Lord Jesus Christ will return to earth. Verse 9:

9 Even [that is to say] him [the Antichrist], whose coming is after the working of Satan with all power and signs and lying wonders,

It may be frightening for us to think about this power of evil growing greater. However, God *letteth* according to His ultimate plan for the restoration of His Creation. Here is our consolation. We know from the Word of God what is the final destiny of evil. Revelation 20:10:

10 And the devil [Satan] that deceived

them was cast into the lake of fire and brimstone, where the beast [the Antichrist] and the false prophet are, and shall be tormented day and night for ever and ever.

He tells about the great divide between those who choose to accept the truth and those who do not. The latter choose to not only ignore it but to remain enemies of God. Like Satan, who is their head, they choose to both deny the truth and fight against it. 2 Thessalonians 2:10:

10 **And with all deceivableness of unrighteousness in them that perish; because they received not the love of the truth, that they might be saved.**

The word *deceivableness* means *the state or extent of one's deception*. Each person has *free will* and can choose to accept or reject God. The deception of mankind has a long history. It began with the father of lies. Today, the majority of people want to be their own god. Not only do they desire to rule themselves, but they want to judge others. Consider the first lie ever told. Genesis 3:4-5:

4 **And the serpent said unto the woman, Ye shall not surely die:** 5 **For God doth**

know that in the day ye eat thereof, then your eyes shall be opened, <u>and ye shall be as gods</u>, knowing good and evil.

These people cannot be reached. They have become impervious to the gospel and commit their time to deluding others. 2 Thessalonians 2:11-12:

11 **And for this cause [reason] God shall send them strong delusion, that they should believe a lie:**

12 **That they all might be damned who believed not the truth, but [instead] had pleasure in unrighteousness.**

There is a consequence for rejecting the righteousness of God when they chose to believe a lie! Like the hardening Pharoah's heart, God sends them a very enticing delusion to strengthen their conviction. They delight in their unrighteousness and want others to do the same. Romans 1:32:

32 **Who knowing the judgment of God, that they which commit such things are worthy of death, <u>not only do the same, but have pleasure in them that do them.</u>**

This is God "Who will have all men to be saved, and

to come unto the knowledge of the truth" (1 Tim. 2:4). Therefore, it would be contrary to His will to delude people. However, He that *letteth* will *let* strong delusion come upon those who reject and continually war against Him.

Those who believe God and accept His gracious offer of salvation by faith can only thank Him for what He has done! So few choose to believe the Gospel of Grace that Paul continues to thank God for those who do believe. 2 Thessalonians 2:13:

> 13 **But we are bound to give thanks alway to God for you, brethren beloved of the Lord, because God hath from the beginning chosen you <u>to salvation through sanctification of the Spirit and belief of the truth</u>:**

While many reject it, these grace believers chose to accept the knowledge of the truth Verse 14:

> 14 **Whereunto [unto which] he [God] called you by our gospel, to the obtaining of the glory of our Lord Jesus Christ.**

The above words refer to *the day of our Lord Jesus Christ* which is the Rapture. Then, our redemption will be complete when we *obtain the glory of our Lord*

Jesus Christ.

Paul continues to encourage them to *stand fast* on the doctrine they received from them whether in person or by letter. Verse 15:

> 15 **Therefore, brethren, stand fast, and hold the traditions which ye have been taught, whether by word, or our epistle.**

Here, the word *traditions* is not the same as *the traditions of men* who created religions. Paul is writing about the *oral tradition.* Paul's teachings were originally carried to others who repeated what they had learned from him in person or from his letters. Like news that is carried from person to person, Paul cautions them not to change it but, instead, hold fast to *the truth.*

Paul concludes this section by speaking about the hope of *His Calling.* Those who are saved by grace will, very soon, be called by Christ to join Him in the air forever. We are to console or comfort each other with this glorious news. For this reason, he calls it the *everlasting consolation.* Verses 16-17:

> 16 **Now our Lord Jesus Christ himself, and God, even our Father, which hath loved us, and hath given us everlasting**

consolation and good hope through grace,

17 Comfort your hearts, and stablish you in every good word and work.

Grace believers are called the Body of Christ for a reason. We are secure in His Beloved Son Who is our Head. As we struggle on earth, we must look forward to what Paul calls our *everlasting consolation.* With this wonderful news, console each other, comfort each other, and continue *in every good word and work . . .* while we await *His Calling.*

9

2 Thessalonians 3

Paul brings this letter to a conclusion with personal requests and well-wishes. 2 Thessalonians 3:1-2:

1 Finally, brethren, pray for us, that the word of the Lord may have free course, and be glorified, even as it is with you:

2 And that we may be delivered from unreasonable and wicked men: for all men have not faith.

He and his company are not immune from the effects of the opposition. Therefore, he asks for their prayers.

Think about the *faithfulness of the Lord*. He is *immovable in His promises*. It is He Who will establish us and keep us from evil. Verses 3-4:

> **3 But the Lord is faithful, who [He] shall stablish you, and keep you from evil.**

> **4 And we have confidence in the Lord touching [concerning] you, that ye both do and will do the things which we command you.**

Paul is confident the Thessalonians will continue to do all they have been taught. God will fill their hearts with *His love* which transcends human understanding. While doing this, they are to be patient. It is a process and, like them, we too are to patiently wait for God to fulfill His promise. Verse 5:

> **5 And the Lord direct your hearts into the love of God, and into the patient waiting for Christ.**

To be clear, *being holy* means *to be separated*. We are to be separated from the world and separated to God. Paul wants us to remain firm in his teachings and to distance ourselves from the ways of the world as well as from those who are worldly. Verse 6:

> **6 Now we command you, brethren, in the name of our Lord Jesus Christ, that**

ye withdraw yourselves from every brother that walketh disorderly, and not after the tradition [teaching] which he received of [from] us.

When they taught the Thessalonians in person, Paul and his companions set themselves as examples. They worked for their livelihood so as not to be a burden to them. Verses 7-8:

7 For yourselves know how ye ought to [should] follow us: for we behaved not ourselves disorderly among you;

8 Neither did we eat any man's bread for nought [nothing]; but wrought [worked] with labour and travail night and day, that we might not be chargeable [owe anything] to any of you:

It was important that Paul's message be given as a gift and not seen as either pay or reward. They could have invoked apostolic authority but instead voluntarily made themselves examples. Verse 9:

9 Not because we have not power, but to make ourselves an ensample [example] unto you to follow us.

There were some who misapplied Paul's teachings of the coming Rapture. They did not work and, unlike Paul, depended on the generosity of other believers. We might say some had become loafers and, in their idleness, they were gossipers and busybodies. Verses 10-11:

> 10 **For even when we were with you, this we commanded you, that if any would not work, [then] neither should he eat.**
>
> 11 **For we hear that there are some which walk among you disorderly, working not at all, but are busybodies.**

All believers should work and support themselves. Verses 12-13:

> 12 **Now them that are such we command and exhort by our Lord Jesus Christ, that with quietness they work, and eat their own bread.**
>
> 13 **But ye, brethren, be not weary in well doing.**

Furthermore, they should not grow tired of good works.

What about those who do not follow his instructions? Here is how they should be handled. Verses 14-15:

14 And if any man obey not our word by this epistle, note that man, and have no company with him, that he may be ashamed.

15 Yet count him not as an enemy, but admonish him as a brother.

They are not to be considered an enemy but must be excluded from fellowship until they regret their actions. It is a form of teaching by a consequence of action. The word *admonish* is perhaps milder than most may think. It means *to warn or notify of a fault* and *to reprove with mildness.* When Paul admonished certain believers, he would later inquire as to their progress out of his concern for them. This is a way to correct wayward believers with the purpose of later reuniting them to fellowship.

The Apostle Paul closes this letter with a blessing and assurance of its authenticity. He does this by applying his own signature to attest to its validity. Verses 16-17:

16 Now the Lord of peace himself give

you peace always by all means. The Lord be with you all.

17 The salutation of Paul <u>with mine own hand</u>, which is the token in every epistle: so I write.

He concludes his letter with this assertion. As grace believers, we are confident of our past, present, and future because of God's wonderful grace. Verse 18:

18 The grace of our Lord Jesus Christ be with you all. Amen.

Epilogue

Today, our lives seem surrounded by uncertainty. This is not unlike what the Thessalonians were experiencing. Paul's letters were intended to encourage these grace believers who were also awaiting *His Calling*. The trials and afflictions they suffered are very much like our own. In this epilogue, I would like to make a few observations regarding this similarity. Each believer is to apply what they learn from God's Word. Here is my personal application from what I learned from Thessalonians.

Every grace believer should be confident that our salvation is complete at the time we believed the Gospel of Grace. We have eternal security. We did nothing to earn our salvation and we can do nothing to lose it. The process of our redemption is only partially complete. Again, we must not confuse this with our salvation as the price has been paid. We bought, paid for, and now belong to God. The first part of our redemption was completed the moment we believed. Spiritually, we are *in Christ* Who is seated beside God the Father in heaven. However, we still remain in our physical bodies – our sinful flesh. The completion of our redemption is guaranteed by the holy Spirit of Promise. Ephesians 1:13-14:

> **13 In whom ye also trusted, after that ye heard the word of truth, the gospel of your salvation: in whom also after that ye believed, <u>ye were sealed with that holy Spirit of promise,</u>**

> **14 Which is the earnest of our inheritance <u>until the redemption of the purchased possession,</u> unto the praise of <u>his glory.</u>**

This *redemption of the purchased possession* will take place at *His Calling*–the Rapture–which is our *blessed hope*. That, my friend, is great news!

I see the process of our redemption happening in three steps. The first step is finished and it guarantees the remaining two steps will be completed. That was our *justification* and it occurred immediately upon our salvation. The word *justification* means that we were declared *not guilty* of all our sins–past, present, and future. Romans 3:22-24:

82

22 Even <u>the righteousness of God which is by faith of Jesus Christ unto all and upon all them that believe</u>: for there is no difference:

23 For all have sinned, and come short of the glory of God;

24 <u>Being justified freely by his grace through the redemption that is in Christ Jesus:</u>

It is important you see this. Our *justification* is complete! It was completed by God and cannot be undone. We have *the righteousness of God which is by faith of Jesus Christ unto all and upon all them that believe* (v. 22).

The second process is *sanctification* which is our *separation* from the world. Think of all of Paul's letters where he instructs the believers to avoid, abstain, or keep away worldly sins and pleasures. Anything that is said to be *holy* or *sanctified* belongs to or is dedicated to God. As grace believers and members of His family, we are to walk worthy of *His Calling*. We should see *sanctification* as a process whereby God *conforms us into the image of His Son*. This is not an accident. This is not unexpected. God intended this in advance! Romans 8:28-30:

28 And we know that all things work together for good to them that love God,
to them who are the called according to
his purpose.

29 For whom he did foreknow, he also
did predestinate <u>to be conformed to the
image of his Son</u>, that he might be the
firstborn among many brethren.

30 Moreover whom he did predestinate,
them he also called: <u>and whom he
called, them he also justified: and
whom he justified, them he also glori-
fied</u>.

In verse 30 above, Paul mentions the third process of our redemption which is called *glorification*.
This occurs when we receive our new body like the
glorified body of Christ Himself. When does this
happen? It happens at *His Calling*–the Rapture. Philippians 3:20-21:

20 For our conversation is in heaven;
from whence also we look for the Sav-
iour, the Lord Jesus Christ:

21 <u>Who shall change our vile body, that
it may be fashioned like unto his</u>

glorious body, according to the working whereby he is able even to subdue all things unto himself.

As we wait for *His Calling,* our conversation or our manner of living should be worthy. How is this to be done? God wants His children to walk holy or separate from the world. This means being living apart from everything that is not of God; everything that is worldly sin. Paul provides a list in his letter to the Galatians of what he considers to be "of the world." Galatians 5:19-21:

> 19 **Now the works of the flesh are manifest [made known], which are these; Adultery, fornication, uncleanness, lasciviousness,** 20 **Idolatry, witchcraft, hatred, variance, emulations, wrath, strife, seditions, heresies,** 21 **Envyings, murders, drunkenness, revellings, and such like . . .**

During this process of sanctifying or separating from the world, it will raise the attention of others as well as the powers and principalities. The latter are the source of our sorrows and afflictions. These are the same sorrows and afflictions that the Lord Jesus Christ experienced during His earthly ministry. 2 Timothy 3:12:

12 **Yea, and <u>all that will live godly in Christ Jesus shall suffer persecution</u>.**

Allow me to pose some questions. The first question has to do with our *justification*. After hearing the gospel of our salvation, we believed. When we believed, we were immediately *justified*–pronounced *not guilty*. This was an immediate action which was completed by God and He placed us *in Christ*. What did we do to earn our *justification?* The answer to this question is easy. We do nothing. It is Christ Who did everything for those who believe and to which we can add nothing!

Stay with me on this. We are going to jump to the last process which is *glorification*. We know that those who were purchased by His blood will receive glorified bodies like Christ at *His Calling*. What must we do to participate in the process of our *glorification?* Look, again, at Romans 8:30 shown above. We must answer that *those whom He justified, those He also glorified.* There are other verses we could use to support this conclusion. However, it appears that we play no part in our *glorification!* So far, we see that it is God Who has done it all to both *justify* grace believers as well as *glorify* them. Now, we can ask the final question. What part do we play in our *sanctification?*

This answer is important for those of us who struggle in the flesh. Paul, who is the Apostle to the Gentiles, was not immune to this struggle. In Romans 7, he discusses the turmoil within us–between our spirit which is good and our flesh which is evil. Here is just a portion. Romans 7:14-20:

> 14 **For we know that the law is spiritual: but I am carnal [in the flesh], sold under sin. 15 For that which I do I allow not: for what I would [do], that do I not; but what I hate, that do I. 16 If then I do that which I would not, I consent unto the law that it is good.**

> 17 **Now then it is no more I that do it, but sin that dwelleth in me. 18 For I know that in me (that is, in my flesh,) dwelleth no good thing: for to will [the desire to do good] is present with me; but how to perform that which is good I find not. 19 For the good that I would [desire to do] I do not: but the evil which I would [desire] not [to do], that I do.**

> 20 **Now if I do that I would [desire] not, it is no more I that do it, but sin that dwelleth in me.**

What Paul wants to do, he does not do. That which he does not want to do, he does. He attributes the cause of this to sin which is from our flesh. It may appear that God has left us alone to deal with this inner conflict, but this is far from the case.

All believers suffer from this battle of the will. For this reason, Paul writes instructions to grace believers who are dealing with this very challenge. Let us finish by look at several verses:

1 Thessalonians 5:23:

> 23 And <u>the very God of peace sanctify you wholly</u> [completely]; and I pray God your whole spirit and soul and body be preserved blameless unto the coming of our Lord Jesus Christ.

1 Corinthians 6:11:

> 11 And such were some of you: <u>but ye are washed, but ye are sanctified, but ye are justified in the name of the Lord Jesus</u>, and by the Spirit of our God.

1 Corinthians 1:2:

> 2 <u>Unto the church of God</u> which is at

Corinth, <u>to them that are sanctified in Christ Jesus</u>, called to be saints, with all that in every place call upon the name of Jesus Christ our Lord, both theirs and ours:

1 Corinthians 1:30-31:

30 But of him are ye in Christ Jesus, who of <u>God is made unto us wisdom, and righteousness, and sanctification, and redemption</u>:

31 That, according as it is written, <u>He that glorieth, let him glory in the Lord.</u>

1 Thessalonians 5:23-24:

23 And <u>the very God of peace sanctify you wholly</u>; and I pray God your whole spirit and soul and body be preserved blameless unto the coming of our Lord Jesus Christ.

24 <u>Faithful is he that calleth you, who also will do it.</u>

2 Thessalonians 2:13-14:

13 But we are bound to give thanks alway to God for you, brethren beloved of the Lord, because God hath from the beginning chosen you to salvation through sanctification of the Spirit and belief of the truth:

14 Whereunto he called you by our gospel, to the obtaining of the glory of our Lord Jesus Christ.

Some may think that I am making a huge leap here, but I am confident that He Who *justified me in Christ* is the same Who will *glorify me in Christ.* Let us draw a conclusion. He Who will *glorify me in Christ* is, at this present time, *sanctifying me in Christ* also!

As we await *His Appearing* we are to lead lives worthy of *His Calling.* In most of his letters, Paul instructs that we should avoid sin but also any appearance of sin for our testimony. Finally, he tells us that we should be filled with joy and comfort one another. 1 Thessalonians 4:16-18:

16 For the Lord himself shall descend from heaven with a shout, with the voice of the archangel, and with the trump of God: and the dead in Christ shall rise first:

17 Then we which are alive and remain shall be caught up together with them in the clouds, to meet the Lord in the air: and so shall we ever be with the Lord.

18 Wherefore comfort one another with these words.

Therefore, knowing that the completion of our redemption draws near, we should remember these words. 2 Thessalonians 2:16-17:

16 Now our Lord Jesus Christ himself, and God, even our Father, which hath loved us, and hath given us everlasting consolation and good hope through grace,

17 Comfort your hearts, and stablish you [yourselves] in every good word and work.

— Dr. David Alan Greene

Other GraceWord Publications

<u>In English:</u>

1st Corinthians: Dispensationally Considered
1st & 2nd Thessalonians: Dispensationally Con.
1st & 2nd Timothy & Titus: Dispensationally Con.
2nd Corinthians: Dispensationally Considered
Acts: Dispensationally Considered
Colossians & Philemon: Dispensationally Con.
Ephesians: Dispensationally Considered
Galatians: Dispensationally Considered
Hebrews: Dispensationally Considered
How Am I Wired?
Letters To Theophilus
Philippians: Dispensationally Considered
Romans: Dispensationally Considered
The Glorious Destiny Of Israel
The Hidden Gospel
The Seven Hebrew Epistles: Dispensationally Con.
Two Distinct Gospel Messages Of The New Test.

<u>En español:</u>

Cartas A Teófilo
Efesios: Dispensacionalmente considerado
El evangelio Oculto: Una vez fue un misterio . . .

About The Author

Dr. David Alan Greene has over thirty-five years of experience as an insurance agent selling both property and casualty as well as life insurance. During his career, he taught and explained the content and meaning of policies to his clients. Now retired, he devotes much of his time to teaching the Bible.

He obtained his Bachelor of Theology, Master of Biblical Studies, and Ph.D. in Biblical Studies from Evangelical Theological Seminary where he holds the position of Dean of Graduate Studies. He also holds a Ph.D. in Christian Counseling. He has written numerous biblical commentaries and books on rightly dividing the Word of Truth.

www.ingramcontent.com/pod-product-compliance
Lightning Source LLC
Chambersburg PA
CBHW070754120626
46557CB00002B/587